DREAM JOBS
If You Like
DINOSAURS

by Amie Jane Leavitt

CAPSTONE PRESS
a capstone imprint

Capstone Captivate is published by Capstone Press, an imprint of Capstone.
1710 Roe Crest Drive
North Mankato, Minnesota 56003
www.capstonepub.com

Copyright © 2021 by Capstone. All rights reserved. No part of this publication may be reproduced in whole or in part, or stored in a retrieval system, or transmitted in any form or by any means, electronic, mechanical, photocopying, recording, or otherwise, without written permission of the publisher.

Library of Congress Cataloging-in-Publication Data is available on the Library of Congress website.
ISBN: 978-1-4966-8399-1 (library binding)
ISBN: 978-1-4966-8450-9 (eBook PDF)

Summary: Wouldn't it be cool to have a job working with or around the things you love? Fascinated by dinosaurs? Perhaps a career in paleontology is something you would dig! Readers will discover the possibilities of careers working with dinosaurs.

Image Credits
Getty Images: Hill Street Studios, 6, Oli Scarff, 14, TORSTEN BLACKWOOD, 15; iStockphoto: abeadev, Cover, benedek, 4, michaeljung, 23, narvikk, 17, ollirg, 7, Photoshopix, 22, rkristoffersen, Cover, Silvrshootr, 16, williamhc, 21; Newscom: MILBERT O. BROWN/KRT, 20; Shutterstock: AmeliAU, back cover, 11, Gorodenkoff, 13, Impact Photography, 10, iofoto, 28, MIKHAIL GRACHIKOV, Cover, Nor Gal, 26, piosi, 18, Radu Bercan, 8, vitstudio, 12, Vorobiov Oleksii 8, 24, Welly Saikat, 19

Editorial Credits
Editor: Heather Williams; Designer: Sara Radka; Media Researcher: Morgan Walters; Production Specialist: Spencer Rosio

All internet sites appearing in back matter were available and accurate when this book was sent to press.

Printed in the United States
PA117

Table of Contents

Paleontologist 4
College Professor 6
Science Museum Curator 8
TV/Movie Researcher 10
Stem Cell Scientist 12
Robotics Engineer 14
National Park Ranger 16
Ornithologist 18
Paleobotanist 20
Paleontological Monitor 22
Scientific Illustrator 24
Dino Theme Park Worker 26
Author 28
    Glossary 30
    Read More 31
    Internet Sites 31
    Index 32

Words in **bold** are in the glossary.

There are millions of jobs in the world. Only a few of them are dream jobs. A dream job might not make you rich or famous. But you'll be excited to go to work every day. If you love playing with, drawing, or reading about dinosaurs, one of these might be your dream job!

Paleontologists use tools to scrape away dirt and rock to uncover fossils.

Paleontologist

Dinosaurs lived on Earth millions of years ago. They are **extinct**. So how do we know anything about them? We learn about them from scientists called **paleontologists**. Paleontologists study life from long ago. They find and study **fossils**.

On the Job

Paleontologists work at **dig sites**, in **labs**, and at museums. They hunt and dig for fossils at dig sites. This exciting work must be done very carefully. The fossils can't be removed quickly. They could break. Fossils are taken to a lab and studied. Some show the remains of tiny living things. Others are made up of many large pieces. They fit together to show the remains of large dinosaurs. Paleontologists learn about Earth's history by studying fossils.

> **FUN FACT**
> The word *fossil* comes from the Latin word *fossus*, which means "dug up."

Pay Range

Average salary = $58,000 to $64,000 per year.

Education and Skills

Paleontologists go to college for six to eight years. They study geology and natural sciences. They use special tools, such as chisels and rock hammers. These chip rock away from fossils. Brushes gently wipe away dust. Dinosaurs are often found far away from big cities. Paleontologists can spend months on a dig site. They camp nearby.

Students who wish to become paleontologists work with professors who are experts on fossils.

College Professor

Some paleontologists spend all day at dig sites. Others teach at colleges and universities. These professors teach students about the world during the time of the dinosaurs.

On the Job

Paleontology professors teach students in classrooms and in labs. In the lab, they can study fossils with students. Some take students into the field to see how fossils are removed from the earth.

Pay Range

Average salary = $40,000 to $60,000 per year.

Education and Skills

Paleontology professors go to college for six to eight years. They study geology or biology. They read many books and articles. Professors must be patient and pay attention to detail. They must be in good physical shape to work long hours on dig sites.

FUN FACT

The biggest dinosaur found so far is the Patagotitan. It was discovered in Argentina. It is 120 feet (37 meters) long. That is nearly half the length of an American football field. It would have weighed more than 70 tons (64 metric tons). That is about the weight of 35 small cars!

Paleontology professors often take their students to dig sites so they can get hands-on experience.

Science museum curators create dinosaur displays that are exciting and educational.

Science Museum Curator

There are many types of science museums. Some focus on outer space or animals. Some focus on dinosaurs. Curators run museums. They choose the objects that are brought into the museum. Then they take care of the objects.

On the Job

Curators work with the **donors** who give or sell things to the museum. They keep lists of all the objects in the museum and where they are kept. This is called cataloging. Curators must make sure objects are stored carefully. Putting a tiny fossil under a huge one would be a bad idea. The small one would get crushed! Curators may also set up the museum's **exhibits**. They decide the theme and what will be displayed. Curators give talks to museum visitors.

Pay Range

Average salary = $46,000 per year.

Education and Skills

Many museum curators go to college for four to eight years. They take classes on how to care for museum objects. They also may study geology and paleontology. Curators pay attention to details. They enjoy talking to people. They use computers to help them catalog.

FUN FACT

Sue the T-Rex is the largest and most complete Tyrannosaurus rex skeleton in the world. She is 40 feet (12 m) long and 13 feet (3.9 m) tall. She is displayed at the Field Museum in downtown Chicago, Illinois.

Well-researched shows and movies allow young dinosaur fans to learn and have fun at the same time.

TV/Movie Researcher

Have you ever watched a TV show about dinosaurs? Or a **documentary** about a dinosaur dig? Maybe you've seen a movie about dinosaurs brought to life. The people who make these shows and movies get help from researchers. These fact finders make sure the dinosaur details are correct.

On the Job

Researchers start out with questions. *What did the Brontosaurus eat? How did the Tyrannosaurus rex run? How many types of dinosaurs could fly?* Then they find the answers. They read about dinosaurs. They talk with experts. Then they share what they've learned with directors and screenwriters. This information makes the film or show seem more real.

> **FUN FACT**
> After the movie *Jurassic Park* came out in 1993, more people enrolled in university paleontology programs.

Pay Range

Average salary = $54,000, but it can be as high as $78,000, based on location and experience.

Education and Skills

Most researchers go to college. They might study science, English, or journalism. Researchers like asking questions and hunting for answers. They know how to find information in the library and online.

TV and movie researchers look at dinosaur drawings and read books about dinosaurs and their habitats.

Stem Cell Scientist

What if dinosaurs could be brought back from extinction? That might sound like a science fiction story. But some scientists have been studying this idea for years. They are called stem **cell** scientists.

On the Job

Stem cell scientists work with stem cells. These are special cells. They can turn into muscle cells, brain cells, or skin cells. Some scientists believe putting dinosaur **DNA** into a stem cell would make dinosaur cells. But no dinosaur DNA has been found yet. Fossils do not contain DNA. Stem cell scientists work in labs using microscopes and computers.

DNA inside a cell looks like a twisted ladder.

Pay Range

Average salary = $77,000 per year.

Education and Skills

Stem cell scientists have college degrees. They go to school for about eight years. They study biology. They must enjoy spending hours peering into a microscope. They usually work on their own. But they should also like working with others. Teamwork is sometimes needed for experiments.

FUN FACT

In 2003, a type of goat was brought back from extinction. The last goat of that kind had died. But scientists were able to get some of its DNA. That DNA was placed into a stem cell. The cells grew and a goat was born. Sadly, though, the goat had physical problems and lived for just seven minutes. It was the first time that a kind of animal became extinct twice.

Stem cell scientists often work as part of a research team to learn new information about DNA.

Robotic dinosaurs often interact with people at theme parks and live shows.

Robotics Engineer

Robotic dinosaurs are used in films and amusement parks. Small ones are made into toys. They are all created by people called robotics engineers. Engineers are people who design and build things.

On the Job

Robotics engineers might make dinosaurs for a movie or a science museum. First, they sketch out ideas. They answer questions. *How big do I want the dinosaur to be? How should it move? Do I want it to make noises?* They use a computer program to design it. They build a **prototype**. Then a software engineer builds a program. The program is the robot's brain. It tells the robot what to do: roar, walk, swim, or fight. Finally, engineers test the robot. They make sure it works the way it should.

Pay Range

Average salary = $87,000 per year.

Education and Skills

Robotics engineers go to college for four or more years. They study robotics and engineering. Those who make animatronic robots may also study paleontology or biology. They learn about the real creatures.

FUN FACT

The bodies of some robotic dinosaurs are made on 3-D printers. First, the fossil copies are gathered. Then the robotic hardware and software is installed. Finally, with a flip of a switch, the robotic dinosaurs come to life!

Dinosaur robots are designed to look real and give audiences a thrill of excitement.

National Park Ranger

Some dinosaur dig sites in the United States are on public land protected by the government. National park rangers watch over the fossils and **traces**. They keep them safe for future visitors.

On the Job

National park rangers live near or in the park where they work. They keep watch over the grounds. They make sure that no one takes or breaks the fossils. They lead tours. They teach visitors to respect the fossils. They give talks about paleontology.

Park rangers talk with guests about where fossils have been found and how to keep them safe.

A park ranger must be alert and aware of his surroundings when on duty.

Pay Range

Salary ranges by experience, between $33,000 and $47,000 per year.

Education and Skills

Most park rangers have a two- or four-year degree. They study science. They also study travel and recreation. Rangers must enjoy the outdoors. They should like hiking and camping. They must also like working with people and speaking to groups.

FUN FACT

John and Brenda Bell were tourists hiking in Arches National Park in Utah in 2007. They discovered a dinosaur bone that was as tall as some six-year-old kids! The park rangers let the Bells help remove the bone from the rock. The bone was named "Bell's Bone" in their honor.

Ornithologist

Today's birds are related to theropod dinosaurs. Theropods had short arms and walked on their back legs. You might think of birds as living theropods. Scientists who study birds are called ornithologists.

Observing birds in their natural habitat is a big part of an ornithologist's job.

On the Job

Ornithologists are wildlife biologists. They go into nature to study birds. They look through binoculars to watch them fly. They climb trees to see their nests. Ornithologists read about birds and study bird fossils in labs. They compare today's birds with animal and bird fossils. This helps them see how birds have changed. It also helps scientists understand certain dinosaurs.

> **FUN FACT**
> The first dinosaur fossil with feathers was found in China in 1996. Since then, more than 50 new feathered dinosaurs have been found in that country.

Pay Range

Average salary = $68,000 per year.

Education and Skills

Ornithologists go to college for four to eight years. They study biology and wildlife zoology. They must like spending time outdoors. They must like to read and study data. Ornithologists often teach what they know to others. Some work at colleges or give public talks. Some even take people on bird-watching tours.

Ornithologists study live birds and sometimes compare them with ancient creatures.

Paleobotanists study delicate plant impressions found in rocks and petrified logs.

Paleobotanist

Animals weren't the only things living millions of years ago. There were also many plants. Plants grew long before dinosaurs roamed the Earth. Paleobotanists study plants that lived long ago.

On the Job

Paleobotanists don't study bone fossils. Plants don't have bones! Instead, they study the **impressions** that plants left behind. They collect and study plant fossils and seed fossils. Fossils show how plants have changed or stayed the same. Some of today's plants are much like those that grew during the time of the dinosaurs. Ferns are called "living fossils." They have not changed much in 350 million years.

Pay Range

Average salary = $40,000 to $60,000 per year.

Education and Skills

Most paleobotanists go to college for six to eight years. They study botany and geology. They enjoy working outdoors and love plants. They must notice details. This helps them compare today's plants with ancient ones.

FUN FACT

Petrified Forest National Park is in northern Arizona. The area is now a hot, dry desert. But it used to be a swampy forest. Over millions of years, the trees petrified. This means they died and turned to stone. The stones are now scattered across the desert sands.

Petrified wood is a tree that has turned into a stone or mineral over millions of years.

Paleontological Monitor

You can't get fossils back once they are gone. Fossils are often found on building sites. Sometimes they are discovered when oil is drilled. Paleontological monitors are called when this happens. They make sure the fossils are safely removed.

Many construction sites are supervised by a paleontological monitor who makes sure no harm comes to nearby fossils.

On the Job

Paleontological monitors work for the government or for companies. They make sure laws protecting fossils are followed. They put on a hard hat and climb down into sites. They watch as fossils are removed. Or they help remove fossils themselves.

> **FUN FACT**
> In June 2019, construction workers in Colorado found an amazing fossil. It was a 68-million-year-old adult Triceratops!

Pay Range

Average salary = $43,000 per year.

Education and Skills

Most paleontological environmental monitors go to college. They study geology or paleontology. Some do not go to college. They learn on the job. They work with paleontologists to learn how to remove fossils. Paleontological monitors are organized and good at talking with people. They also understand construction and other types of work that might affect fossils.

Paleontological monitors and workers team up to make a plan that takes the job, as well as the safety of fossils, into consideration.

A scientific illustrator must have careful attention to detail.

Scientific Illustrator

Science books are filled with pictures of dinosaurs. They are shown swimming in the sea, flying in the sky, and walking through swamps. But no one has ever seen a dinosaur in real life. How did we get these images? A special kind of artist called a scientific illustrator creates them. Their artwork mixes facts and imagination.

On the Job

Scientific illustrators learn about dinosaurs in articles and books. They study fossils. They talk to paleontologists. Then they piece together this information. Their drawings show what dinosaurs could have looked like. Scientific illustrators must also learn about the places where the animals lived. That way, they can draw the animals in their natural surroundings.

FUN FACT

Scientific illustrations of dinosaurs often change over time. New discoveries are made. The Tyrannosaurus rex is one example. Scientists now believe this beast was partially covered with feathers. Today's Tyrannosaurus rex pictures look a lot different from those drawn in the past.

Pay Range

Average salary = $56,000 per year.

Education and Skills

Scientific illustrators study art and science in college. They must know how to draw and paint. Their art must be as factual as possible. So they must know about science too. Some use pen and paper to draw. Others create digital art using electronic tablets and computers.

Dino Theme Park Worker

What would it be like to work alongside roaring dinosaurs all day? Scary? Not at all. These dinosaurs aren't real! They're in dinosaur-themed amusement parks. People who work at these parks travel back to the Jurassic era every day.

Dino theme park workers help children have fun while learning about dinosaurs.

On the Job

Dino theme parks offer many jobs. Workers sell tickets. They keep the park clean. They cook food. They work in gift shops. Some dino parks have rides. Workers run the rides and make sure they're safe. Some workers dress up in costumes. They might walk around the park as dino wranglers. They might even dress as dinosaurs!

Pay Range

Average salary = $24,000 per year.

Education and Skills

Theme park workers are trained on the job. They must like working with people. Guests are an important part of a theme park. Few theme park jobs are desk jobs. Theme park workers spend long hours on their feet. They must be willing to learn many different roles.

FUN FACT

The first dinosaur park in the world was the Crystal Palace Dinosaurs in London, England. It opened in 1854. It was home to the world's first dinosaur sculptures. They were created by the artist Benjamin Waterhouse Hawkins. Visitors to London can still view these works of art today.

Authors often visit schools and public libraries to read their work to children.

Author

Do an internet search for "dinosaur books." There are thousands of titles to read. Many authors write about topics like dinosaurs. They write fiction stories about dinosaur characters. They write stories about people who live with dinosaurs. They also write nonfiction books filled with facts.

On the Job

Some authors start with an idea for a dinosaur book. Others are given an assignment. Authors research their topic to learn more about it. They read books and articles. They also talk to paleontologists. They may visit museums and look at fossils. Then they start to write. Authors rewrite many times before they are finished. It can take a number of years to complete one book.

Pay Range

Salary varies greatly, depending upon the author. The average is about $62,000 per year.

Education and Skills

Some authors have college degrees. Others do not. Authors must love to read and write. They must be creative to come up with good ideas. Authors must also be willing to work long hours. They must be flexible and understand that not everyone will love their ideas. Most authors write on computers.

> **FUN FACT**
>
> Author Michael Crichton wrote the book *Jurassic Park* in 1990. In 1993, it was turned into one of the most popular dinosaur-themed movies of all time. The film and its four sequels have made almost $5 billion worldwide.

Glossary

cell (SEL)—the basic part of an animal or plant that is so small you can't see it without a microscope

dig site (DIG SITE)—a place where scientists remove dinosaur fossils

DNA (dee-en-AY)—material in cells that gives people their individual characteristics

documentary (dahk-yuh-MEN-tuh-ree)—movie or TV program about real situations and people

donor (DOH-nuhr)—a person who gives money or objects

exhibit (ig-ZI-buht)—a display that shows something to the public

extinct (ik-STINGKT)—no longer living

fossil (FAH-suhl)—the remains or traces of plants and animals that are preserved as rock

impression (im-PRESH-uhn)—a marking from a branch, leaf, or stem that is left on the surface of a rock

lab (LAB)—a place for scientific experiments

prototype (PROH-tuh-tipe)—the first version of an invention that tests an idea to see if it will work

robotic (roh-BAHT-ick)—relating to machines that perform tasks for humans

trace (TRAYSS)—evidence of dinosaurs or other prehistoric living things that were not actually part of the thing itself, such as footprints or imprints of feathers or skin preserved in rock

Read More

Abbott, Simon. *100 Questions About Dinosaurs.* White Plains, NY: Peter Pauper Press, 2018.

Dinosaurs: A Visual Encyclopedia. New York: DK Publishing/Penguin Random House, 2018.

Garnett, Jaye. *Smithsonian Kids: Digging for Dinosaurs.* Rolling Meadows, IL: Cottage Door Press, 2017.

Sampson, Scott D. *You Can Be a Paleontologist: Discovering Dinosaurs with Dr. Scott.* Washington, D.C.: National Geographic, 2017.

Internet Sites

Dinosaurs
https://www.ducksters.com/animals/dinosaurs.php

Dinosaurs 101
https://youtu.be/e5BFR-E-ae0

Dinosaurs for Kids
http://www.sciencekids.co.nz/dinosaurs.html

Junior Paleontologist
https://www.nps.gov/subjects/fossils/junior-paleontologist.htm

Paleontology: The Big Dig
https://www.amnh.org/explore/ology/paleontology

Index

art, 25, 27
authors, 28–29

biology, 7, 13, 15, 19
botany, 21

college professors, 6–7
computers, 9, 12, 14, 25, 29

dig sites, 5, 6, 7, 16
dino theme park
 workers, 26–27
DNA, 12, 13

engineering, 15
exhibits, 9

fossils, 4, 5, 6, 9, 12, 15, 16, 19, 20, 22, 23, 25, 29

geology, 5, 7, 9, 21, 23

journalism, 11
Jurassic Park, 11, 29

labs, 5, 6

museums, 5, 8, 9, 14, 29

national park ranger, 16–17

ornithologists, 18–19

paleobotanists, 20–21
paleontological
 monitors, 22–23
paleontologists, 4–5, 6, 7, 25, 29

robotics engineers, 14–15

science museum curators, 8–9
scientific illustrators, 24–25
stem cell scientists, 12–13

tools, 5
TV/movie researchers, 10–11